# What Do You Know About the
# Water Cycle?

press.
New York

Gillian Gosman

Published in 2014 by The Rosen Publishing Group, Inc.
29 East 21st Street, New York, NY 10010

First Edition

Editor: Jennifer Way
Book Design: Kate Laczynski

Photo Credits: Cover Altrendo Travel/Altrendo/Getty Images; cover interior graphic risteski goce/Shutterstock.com; p. 5 © iStockphoto.com/magaliB; p. 6 Monkey Business/Thinkstock; p. 7 Dreamframer/Shutterstock.com; p. 8 John A. Anderson/Shutterstock.com; pp. 9, 20, 21 © iStockphoto/Thinkstock; p. 10 by Michelle Lala Clark Photography; p. 11 Jupiterimages/Photos.com/Thinkstock; p. 12 Fernando Jose Vasconcelos Soares/Shutterstock.com; p. 13 S. J. Krasemann/Peter Arnold/Getty Images; pp. 14–15 tonyz20/Shutterstock.com; p. 15 HABRDA/Shutterstock.com; p. 16 Volodymyr Goinyk/Shutterstock.com; p. 17 IrinaK/Shutterstock.com; p. 18 Jupiterimages/Brand X Pictures/Thinkstock; pp. 18–19 (top) Goodshoot/Thinkstock; pp. 18–19 (bottom) Teresatky/Shutterstock.com; p. 22 Jupiterimages/Comstock/Thinkstock.

Gosman, Gillian.
 What do you know about the water cycle? / by Gillian Gosman. — 1st ed.
   p. cm. — (20 questions: earth science)
Includes index.
ISBN 978-1-4488-9697-4 (library binding) — ISBN 978-1-4488-9852-7 (pbk.) — ISBN 978-1-4488-9853-4 (6-pack)
1. Hydrologic cycle. 2. Weather. 3. Landforms. I. Title.
GB848.G67 2013
551.48—dc23
                              2012028456

Manufactured in the United States of America

CPSIA Compliance Information: Batch #S13PK5: For Further Information contact Rosen Publishing, New York, New York at 1-800-237-9932

# Contents

# What Do You Know About the Water Cycle?

Water is a wonderful thing! It can be found as all three states of matter. As water, it is a liquid. As ice, it is a solid. Water **vapor** is a gas. You can change water from one state to the next at home by putting water in the freezer to make ice or by heating water on the stove to make water vapor. These changes also take place in nature through the steps of the water cycle.

In this book, we will be exploring the water cycle. We will learn about the basic stages of the water cycle and about weather, landforms, and our role in this never-ending cycle.

This diagram shows how water moves through the stages of the water cycle.

Cloud formation

Precipitation

Evaporation

Evaporation

Runoff

Groundwater

Collection
and storage

# 1. What is a cycle?

We say that water travels through a cycle, but what is a cycle? A cycle is a series of events that repeats over and over. At any one moment in time, there is water in each step of the cycle, which is in turn in the process of moving to another stage in the cycle.

Rain is an example of one of the stages of the water cycle.

## 2. Where does water come from?

The water cycle has no beginning and no end. Water has been moving through the water cycle since the beginning of Earth's history. The same water that flowed in rivers and streams when dinosaurs walked Earth is around today, falling from the sky as rain, flowing in rivers, and forming clouds overhead.

The water flowing over this waterfall has always existed on Earth in one form or another!

## 3. What is evaporation?

**Evaporation** is one event in the water cycle. It is the process by which water changes from a liquid to a vapor.

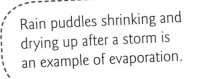

Rain puddles shrinking and drying up after a storm is an example of evaporation.

## 4. What are examples of evaporation?

Sometimes you see evaporation as steam rising from a lake. More often, water vapor can be felt but not seen. When there is a lot of water vapor in the air around us, we say it is humid.

## 5. What is the Sun's role in the water cycle?

Evaporation takes place when water is heated. Heat weakens the bonds that hold the water **molecules** together until they break. In nature, this heat is provided by the Sun. The Sun's heat warms the water in puddles, lakes, rivers, streams, and oceans. The water evaporates and enters Earth's **atmosphere** as water vapor.

The Sun's heat causes evaporation on bodies of water throughout the day.

## 6. What is transpiration?

People, animals, and plants are all part of the water cycle because they all release water into the atmosphere. Humans perspire, or sweat, to stay cool, and plants **transpire**. Transpiration is the process by which water is released from a plant's leaves and evaporates into the atmosphere.

Fog is an example of condensation. Water vapor in the air has cooled and formed water droplets in the air.

CONDENSATION

Water vapor remains a vapor as long as it is warm. As water vapor cools, the gas returns to liquid form. This process is called **condensation**.

**8.** What are examples of condensation?

You can see condensation in your own kitchen. Fill a glass with ice-cold water. Set it on the counter. Watch as beads of water form on the outside of the glass. The cold glass cooled the air around it, and the water vapor in the air condensed on the surface of the glass.

## 9. How do clouds form?

Water vapor is lighter than air. When water evaporates into water vapor, it rises. As water vapor rises high up into the atmosphere, it cools. As the vapor cools, the bonds that hold the molecules together grow stronger. The vapor condenses and forms clouds.

This airplane is flying through cumulus clouds.

**10.** What kinds of clouds are there?

There are many kinds of clouds. They are given Latin names that describe both their appearance and their places in the sky. For example, cumulus clouds look like fluffy balls of cotton. Clouds with "cirrus" in their names are high in the atmosphere and look like wispy strands of hair. Fog is actually a cloud, too! It is a cloud that forms close to the ground.

13

Clouds are carried across the sky by the movements of air. Sometimes the water droplets in the clouds attach to tiny pieces of dust or salt in the air. These droplets grow heavy. When the droplets get heavy enough, they fall from the cloud. Droplets of water falling from clouds are called **precipitation**.

SNOW

**12.** What kinds of precipitation are there?

The main forms of precipitation are rain, snow, sleet, and hail.

## 13. What determines the type of precipitation that falls?

The temperature determines what type of precipitation falls. If the ground and the air from the cloud to the ground are above 32° F (0° C), precipitation will fall as rain. If the ground or the air between the cloud and the ground is colder than that, then the precipitation can freeze and form freezing rain, snow, sleet, or hail.

Hail forms in clouds high up in the atmosphere where the temperature is below freezing. That is why you might see hail during a summer thunderstorm.

## 14. What is water collection and storage?

When water returns to the ground as precipitation, it flows downhill. **Collection** is when that water comes together to form streams, rivers, lakes, and oceans. **Storage** is the period during which the collected water is kept in a body of water. Water is also stored in **glaciers** and in the ice near the North and South Poles. This stored water will slowly evaporate and continue moving through the water cycle.

This glacier is part of the polar ice stored near the South Pole.

18

Rivers like this one are an example of water being collected and stored.

## 15. What is groundwater?

Water is also stored deep underground. Groundwater is water that has seeped deep down into the ground and collected and stored there.

## 16. Where does drinking water come from?

Many people around the world get their drinking water from the water stored in rivers, lakes, and streams. Other people dig wells deep in the ground to reach groundwater. This freshwater can be used for drinking.

Not all water is naturally good for drinking. People need to drink freshwater because drinking salt water can be harmful.

## 17. What is the difference between freshwater and salt water?

The world's oceans and some lakes are filled with salt water. Rivers and other water sources pick up small amounts of salt and other minerals as they move. When this water flows into the ocean, the salt is deposited there and builds up, making the water salty.

Where freshwater rivers and saltwater oceans meet, **brackish** water can be found. Brackish water can form naturally or be the result of human impact on the **environment**.

Salt water, such as ocean water, is water that contains at least 3.5 percent salt.

Water treatment plants clean our drinking water. From there, it is sent to our homes.

Building cities and streets puts a lot of cement on the ground. This can keep water from flowing into the ground like it normally would.

**18.** How do human activities affect the water cycle?

Wherever people settle, clear land, and build cities, the water cycle is affected. We use a great deal of freshwater. We **pollute** rivers, lakes, and oceans. These actions, along with many others, affect the water cycle every day.

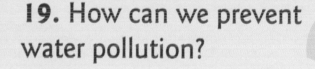

**WATER POLLUTION**

**19.** How can we prevent water pollution?

We can take simple steps every day to prevent water pollution. Use less water. The less water you use, the less water needs to be treated, or cleaned. Do not throw your garbage down the drain, especially things like paint. Avoid using chemicals on your lawn or garden because they can get into the groundwater and enter the water cycle.

## 20. Why is water conservation important?

We should all work to **conserve** water. The human impact on the water cycle is felt all across the world. The damage we do in one place can affect the other side of the planet, and the same is true in reverse. Some parts of the world are facing long, deadly **droughts**. Other areas are facing dangerous weather, such as flooding. Whether the problem is too little water or too much, it is important to use water wisely and to keep it clean.

If you need to water your garden, you can save water by doing it early in the morning or in the evening. Less water is lost to evaporation that way.

**atmosphere** (AT-muh-sfeer)  The gases around an object in space. On Earth this is air.

**brackish** (BRA-kish)  Somewhat salty.

**collection** (kuh-LEK-shun)  When water comes together to form streams, lakes, rivers, and oceans.

**condensation** (kon-den-SAY-shun)  Cooled gas that has turned into drops of liquid.

**conserve** (kun-SERV)  To keep something from being wasted or used up.

**droughts** (DROWTS)  Periods of dryness that hurt crops.

**environment** (en-VY-ern-ment)  Everything that surrounds people and other living things and everything that makes it possible for them to live.

**evaporation** (ih-va-puh-RAY-shun)  When a liquid, such as water, changes to a gas.

**glaciers** (GLAY-shurz)  Large masses of ice that move down mountains or along valleys.

**molecules** (MAH-lih-kyoolz)  Two or more atoms joined together.

**pollute** (puh-LOOT)  To hurt with certain kinds of bad matter.

**precipitation** (preh-sih-pih-TAY-shun)  Any moisture that falls from the sky. Rain and snow are precipitation.

**storage** (STOR-ij)  The period during which collected water is kept in a body of water.

**transpire** (trants-SPY-er)  To evaporate from the leaves and the stems of plants.

**vapor** (VAY-per)  A liquid that has turned into a gas.

# Index

# Websites

Due to the changing nature of Internet links, PowerKids Press has developed an online list of websites related to the subject of this book. This site is updated regularly. Please use this link to access the list:
www.powerkidslinks.com/20es/water/